Snake~Back Solos
SELECTED POEMS, 1969-1977

Quincy Troupe

I. REED BOOKS
285 East 3rd Street
New York, New York 10009

Some of the poems in this volume were published in the following publications:
Sunbury 1, Sunbury 2, Sunbury 3, Black Scholar, Black Creation, Giant Talk, Black World, Encore, Essence, BOPP, Okike, The Town Review, Griefs of Joy, Celebrations, Nimrod, Indigine, Epoch, For Neruda, For Chile.

This project was supported by a small press grant from the New York Council of the Arts.

Printed in the United States of America

I. Reed Books is a division of Reed & Cannon. Main office: 285 East 3rd St., New York City, N.Y. 10009. Order Department: I. Reed Books, 2140 Shattuck Ave., Rm. 311, Berkeley, CA, 94704

Cover painting by Oliver Jackson
Back cover photo by Dawoud Bey

Book Design: Andrea DuFlon Heide

This book is dedicated to Lynne Edwards —
marvelous spirit
marvelous woman
great friend
with deep gratitude and love . . .

CONTENTS

Ash Doors & Juju Guitars

ASH DOORS & JUJU GUITARS

we have come through doors flaming
ashes the sad written legacy
smoldering bones heaped in pyres behind us

& yet campfire blues people singing
softly still under blue black moonlight

ash doors & juju guitars conjurin ancestral flights

sweet memories of shaman juju men
cotton-eyed bands croonin
softly the guitar-woman stroked enjoins

blues chanting mantras across throbbing land

at the flight of sun   light
at the flight of sun   light

UP SUN SOUTH OF ALASKA;
A Short African American History Song
(For My Son, Brandon Troupe)

1.

slit balls hung in southern/american winds then
when drumheads were slit made mum by rum
& songs hung way down
around our ankles bleeding up sun south of alaska
swinging silhouettes picked clean to bone
by black crows
caw caw razor scars black-winged crows ripping
sunset flights of slashing razors
crows crows
blues caw caws & moans
& blues caw caws & moans

then sunsets dangled voices
crowing blues caw caws black crowing razors streak
silhouettes against a frying skillet sky
broken necks & sun-gored bodies blistered in eclipse
hung nails rope burned
into sweet black lives

rip of pendulum razors
lays open the quaking earth of flesh/ moans
from blue-black dues paying women
dropping embryos into quicksand
african secret songs strapped across blood-stained blades
of glittering american razors
songs of sun/down flesh karintha dusk flesh
drug through spit/ripped
bleeding up sun south of alaska
bleeding up sun south of alaska

2.

& crows & razors & ropes & bullets
crows & razors & ropes & bullets
the shared cold legacy
& crazed pale men lassoing the sun out of the sky
& darkness then bleeding up sun south of alaska
crow wings covering the sky & our eyes & their eyes too
eclipsing the face of the sun
now an invisible clock with laser-beamed hands
that are branding rays burning our flesh
reduced over time to bone/dust
kissing stone but the nature of stone
is not moved by the tongue of heat entering
the mouth of our lives — passionate sweet touch of meaning

but still we move through space towards grace
carrying a sphinx in one eye
a guitar in the other knowing that time is always
in the possession of the keeper

3.

so now son black
roll the pages of your american eyes back son
black son roll them back black son american
son way way back son
back before the sun ripped your flesh here
way way back sun
for the pages of your eyes carry the memory son
they are blue-black pages dues pages fingers strumming
music of oral history songs griot songs
african songs
strong black strumming fingers son
american black lives as humming caw caws

black crows transformed into eagles

no matter ripping suns son
no matter slit drums/tongues
we are here son
are sun music spirit son
caw caw blues razors

keepers of secret guitars

THESE CROSSINGS, THESE WORDS
For Pablo Neruda

where will they take us to
these crossings
over rivers of blood-stained words
syllables haphazardly thrown together
as marriages that fall apart
in one day

we have come this far in space
to know nothing of time
of the imprisoning distance travelled
the scab-fleshed hobos passed
we have most times asked nothing

of the mirrors of our own shattered reflections
passing us as lava smoldering in the streets

in our red eyes the guillotine
smile of the hangman
a time-bomb ticking for our hearts
the brain an item bought like so much gooey candy
the laugh a razor's flash
the party time juba
of My Lai's sickening ritual

as american as elvis presley's dead days

& the blood-scarred wind
whipped rag blue squared off with stars
that are silver bullets
& pin-striped with bones of mythologized peppermint
will not hide the corpse-lynched history
hanging there twisting slowly
as a black man's body
screaming through soft magnolia air
over a tear-stained bride's veil
breeze blown & fluttering
as a flopping fish
in a gesture of surrender

12

we have come all this distance in darkness
bomb-flashes guiding our way
speaking of love / of passions instantly eclipsed
to find this corpse of freedom hung & machine-gunned
for the blood of a name beneath a simple word
(& what do we know who have not gone there in truth
of the roots of these flames burning at river-crossings
of the crossbones of our names connecting rivers
of blood beautiful as a fusing coltrane solo?)

& there are times when we see
celluloid phantoms of mediarized lovers
crawling from sockets of cracking up skeletons
posing as cameras & t.v. screens

times still when we stand here
anchored to silence by terror
of our own voice & of the face revealed
in the unclean mirror shattering
our sad-faced children
dragging anchors of this gluttonous
debauchery & of this madness
that continues to last

SNAKE-SONG SLITHERING TOWARDS EVEL

For Evel Knievel

"The United States has not lost a past;
it has lost its future."

—*Octavio Paz*

it is the last bells tolling
of twelve o'clock midnight
of the last year
during the last moments
of disaster/ snake eyes

disaster/ snake eyes

duce game
of snake twins
(eyes locked broken
between parentheses).

in dual deaths
of loaded crap games

two bones over
graveyard green rolling
as in a golf game bold cold toll of snakes
black spots
on paper thin ash white skulls

beyond death
beyond polished bones

snake cold   snake bold

twist double/ time steel
snaking worm moles through dark twelve o'clock
stark midnight pits of tunneled hours   drag
of final years
fearing the final moment

14

of disaster/ snake cross

snake toll

& O the ego strikes cold
bold snakebites
between parentheses

between disasters

snake dark
snakepits bleached white
staked skeletons on sand under sun
millions of ants swarm
from scarfed-out eye sockets
run screaming everywhere
question marks of rib cages
fossilized american bones
everywhere sun bleached

silence everywhere

bones run under scorching sun
alongside snakes slithering creating patterns
on sand belly down zig-zag runs on sand
creating crucifixes of language
as the faith is eaten clean

as wormed flesh of George

Washington/ bridge
falling down watergate(s) flooded
cities gored by their own ignorance
as voices of bleached rib cages speak
wind-sand saws through bones
frictioned clean
by piranha teeth violence
of time's sad language

of mad wars laid bare

15

rattlesnakes amongst the vertebrae
boned terror as silence grips polluted air
hulls of sunken ships
wing spars of crashed airplanes
museum space skeletons of Cape Kennedy
corporate garbage peaks of power dreams
masticated voices
sunken ruins of shrivelled flesh
skulls as bobbing cigarette butts
in stagnant unused coffee cups
pythons of greed crushing
life breath returned to death

snake cold   snake bold
& O sad egos strike bold
cold snakebites
between parentheses

                    between disasters

cobra-blooded
fanging frozen people

it's so coldly muddled
America/ dreaming & screaming
it's so cold-blooded

America now

TODAY'S SUBWAY RIDE

whole 'nother thang goin down
the subway train streakin music
through darkness the way of the trane
the way of the steel wheels lickin & clickin
through snakin holes   moles
two-eyed steel worm moles snakin through
space tight dark   train packin people
sardine can tight   packin people
starin off into space   pit deep black space
elusive-eyed people spacin out on grafitti
that stares back at their own empty eyeballs
elusive as dusk when the dark comes down
elusive as life when death comes down
& everywhere we go headlines
of bizarre madness starin back at us
everywhere we go this pervading sadness
starin back at us
this mad dog american grafitti staring down
at us everywhere we go on subway trains
pee smells assaulting nostrils
blood breaking wine stains everywhere
we go & the subway train floor
finally as dinner table —
our eyeballs rolling across
the gritty floor like bogied marbles

NEW YORK STREETWALKER

under stabbling streetlights
slanting beams of looping lassos
eclipse of sun gored out
under a canopy of breaking darkness
distance & a wheezing soup sky breaks snow
like a pearl-lipped vagina coming
& the moon rolls back behind
menstruating gray clouds on night canvas
like a pearl falling off
a black dress of worn silk

& she walks there like hot ice in heat
or as tonight in frozen razor weather
under ripping hawk of december
breath hung as ice mist
beneath cheap hanging tinsel of christmas
a female santa claus on empty sidestreets
of the worm-eaten big apple
walks snow clouds coughing up her dress
mini-skirted tight above her knees

& cold hugs her shivering poontang
there round & moving in knowing body language
her long sleek legs supple as two pythons
encasing customers
slink down to silver shoes
high-heeled spikes that walk clicking

& with the hawk beaking down heavy
leaving frozen marks upon her bulging cleavage
jingling she shivers on under moon-streetlights
like a ghost stuffing devalued money up her worn womb
smiling lonely at all who come her way
until she drifts away like so many swirling
storms into drifts into freezing snow locked
morning like a pearl-lipped vagina
coming overhead under menstruating soup
snow clouds lights gone out
of her face & the night

NEW YORK CITY BEGGAR

his body held the continence
of a protruding tongue
of a hanged man twisting & turning
in sweltering needle-sharp heat
held the continence
of a jet plane's high propulsion saliva
his body swollen as a toilet stool
packed full of two-day-old shit
warts crawling like frenzied roaches
over his skin of yellow fever
bloated as the graves of earth
or jammed as rivers full
of lynched black bodies —
sores popping open through ventilated
clothing like hungry termites
devouring flesh
the texture of quivering pus

& he looked at me
with the look of a wrung-necked chicken
with that of a somnambulist
blasted by poison of thunderbird wine
storms his eyes streaked red
with crow-wings raking corners
of his peppermint moons
like claws of a rooster

& his fingernails   the color of tadpoles
sought the origin of a 400-year-old itch
which held the history
& secret of crushed indian bones
& of clamoring moaning voices
of unborn black children who were
screaming semen of castrated nigga dicks

& his look held the origin of ashes
the blood-stained legacy of sawdust on the floor
of a butcher
                    & his rasping sawblade voice cutting
held the unmistakeable calligraphy of lepers
who with elephantiasis feet drag themselves across
sword blades of murderous pentagon juntas

(which is the history of reared-back cobra snakes
which is the truth of the game we're in.)

& when he spoke to me
his maggot-swarming words reeking of outhouses
"brother, can you spare a dime?"
his spirit low as coaldust
his energy drained as transparent shells
of sunstricken cockroaches his breath
smelling of rotten fish markets
his teeth looking like chipped tombstones
nicked away in a hurricane of razors
eye heard a fork-tongued capitalist
on wall street fart & croak

(which is the history of reared-back king cobras
which is the truth of the game we're in.)

& when eye walked away with my dime
still chattering in my pocket
he put a halloween leer on me said "thank you,
boss" gave the V for victory/peace sign
cursed under his breath
& left like an apparition flapping
his raggedy black coat
like giant crow wings in the wind

AFTER HEARING A RADIO ANNOUNCEMENT:
A COMMENT ON SOME CONDITIONS

yesterday in new york city
the gravediggers went on strike
& today the undertakers went on strike
because they said of the overwhelming
amount of corpses
(unnecessarily they said because
of wars & stupid killings in the streets
& etcetera & etcetera.)

sweating the world corpses
propped up straight in living room chairs
clogging up rivers   jamming up freeways
stopping up elevators   in the gutters   corpses
everywhere you turn
& the undertakers said that they were
being overworked with all this goddamned killing
going on   said that they couldn't even enjoy
all the money they was making
said that this shit has got to stop

& today eye just heard that
the coffin-makers are waiting in the wings
for their chance to do the same thing
& tomorrow & if things keep going this way
eye expect to hear of the corpses
themselves boycotting death
until things get better
or at least getting themselves
together in sort of union-espousing
self-determination
for better funeral &
burial conditions
or something extraordinarily
heavy like that

NEW YORK BLACK DISCO SCENE; 1976

afro-vogue sleek black high-flown
model types slick purple lips
eyelashes so long they sweep ceilings
stylin is the essence
of these anthracitic men & women
of packaged mannerisms
their midnights deep inside
cold blues
afro-vogue new york disco
syrupy music bright lights

jeweled wings of seraphims
baubles of rhinestones flash long glittering
nails as razors
sharp eyes
weaving cobra rhythms bodies moving inside silk
supple taut movements suggestive
as high-wire tension

afro-disco flights
glitter-glatter symbols computerized
xeroxed people compartmentalized
mirrors gliding through liquid smoke
laviticus
you see there now
the bottom line hanging
latexed women as frozen meat
from goring hooks refrigerated
in deep freeze now their feelings
where reed thin cool black
men sportin french cut
tailored suits / pruned
sideburns / floor-length
leathers / furs
attaché cases stuffed
with credit cards say
"baby, it ain't 'bout
no commitment
but, can I come
home with you tonight?"

here earth smells
have no place or meaning
hear no innovative black language
no human love given
but tongue-in-cheek-chic
fashion plate givenchy / chanel
number five / monsieur rochas
english leather
hear chit-chat of ice-cubes
with no memory of who murdered
fred hampton
snatched away that
beautiful light

here plastic smiles
fuse tinsel feelings
false everyone dances inside
themselves unattached they clock
the slow weave / kinetic shadows
under strobelights hypnotic
pursuit of the elusive
mediarized black
american dream / image somewhere off
in the distance their eyes locked
within the fog of this evening
the kaleidoscope of fractured lights
breaking everything into prisms
somewhere off they doze
beyond the color line beyond
madison avenue drawing boards of fashion
inside neo-zoot suit reality somewhere
off inside themselves
inside creative appearance imagin-
nation / somewhere off inside
narcotized
hedonistic dream fantasies
blasted by alcohol
inside crystal liquid smoke
laviticus   they slow weave frantic
dance the dialectics of fused culture
clockwork orange black america
they become cold cardboard
frigid language of the night
sleek showplace mannequins
in flight / changeable as weather
become the future mutants
that malcolm spoke of

STEEL POLES GIVE BACK NO SWEAT
After Waring Cuney

in new york city people
cop their own posts
underground waiting on subway platforms
lean up against them
claim them as their own
ground & space

while up over ground
winds scrape the back of skies piercing
poles of concrete laced with laughing quicksilver
mirrors square phallic symbols
in their glint
of limp-dick capitalism
repositories for fallen
pigeon shit

below them stoned bums
scrape their lives into asphalt sleep
on sidewalks slow shuffle scabby bruised feet towards terrors
only they know
leaning underground
against graffitied steel subway poles
alone carrying their feverish frenzy
that needed bathing long ago

& so each day here we pass
each other waiting for love to speak
to us to everyone so slow in coming here
to cleanse our needs of these terrible wounds
scraped raw by these clawing days
leaning forward into one another
our lives touching here
these underground steel poles
propping up our bodies
flawed by breath
& annointed with scents
from wherever it is we are coming from

& can feel the flesh rubbing steel
& think the steel flesh
& tell ourselves we are not lonely here
couldn't be lonely
here in this gargantuan city
where steel poles
give back no sweat

SNOW & ICE

ice sheets sweep this slick mirrored darkness
as keys that turn tight trigger brains
of situations
where we move ever so slowly
        so gently into time-spaced agony
bright turning of imagination
so slowly
through revolving doors opening up to enter mountains
where spirits walk voices so slowly swept
by cold breathing fire
        as these elliptical moments of illusion
fragile loves sunk deep in snows as footprints
weak chained black gesticulations
bone bared voices
        chewed skeletal choices
in fangs of vampirish gales
these slivers of raucous laughter
glinting bright as hard polished nails

A SURREALISTIC POEM TO EVERYONE
& NO ONE IN PARTICULAR

high above the ceiling of imagination
crescendo thunderclaps of silence
before lightning a tongue of pearls slashing
the tapestry of God's eye
totemic gongringer of cocaine spells
consummate tapdancer on the holy rings
around saturn
        hydraulic wingbeater
of a dehydrated eagle
laid back soothsayer
who sees the world as one grain of sand
cosmic mindsmoker of the seven skies of dewdrops & doowops
righteous deep sea diver
of the hot sucking womb

this tomb-headed chronicler of the dark
secrets of the vatican
omnipotent court jester
        of the kingdom of novacaine
stomp down choreographer of nod & stumble
junkie ballets
scientific finder of collapsed river veins
molecular rhesus monkey of the ultimate trip of battery acid
peyote sky tripper eater of jagged sharp tin cans
fire swallowing termite of esoteric books
bringer of hot-ice seasons of unknown climates
gri-gri stone eater of broken lightbulbs
bubonic triggerman of no hesitation

out here your test-tube children wearing
uniforms full of worthless medals wearing tight-fitting suits
with buttons popping club-footed dancers
of wet dream midnights

totemic gongringer of cocaine spells

all these desert-fried faces
of sandstorms / chopped iguanas
rattlesnaking eyeballs swarming with garbage
flies sweating speech as buzzsaws of termites
cutting through redwood trees
night-trippers of onion & garlic kisses
toe-tappers of naked nose rubbing eskimos
bellringers of sandpaper pussies
sardine flesh rappers of cat-shit breath

whose eyes gleam sharp as piranha teeth
whose skunk smelling sword blade words reek
of no consequence & nixonian intentions blubberous
jellyfishes of short legs knobby knees
& long flat-footed premonitions

no doubt about it gongringer
the brain of mankind is sometimes a piss
of swiss cheese on the plate of a beggar

FROM RICHMOND COLLEGE, POSTMARKED — MANHATTAN

from this plate-glass window
high above staten island
night closes in on the jugular vein of day
as black paint spreads down over space
of white canvas
squeezing out the life
cycle of day

artificial lights shimmer/ dance
bojangle out of focus
tap-dance across the sound stuffed with slow moving ships
as the verranzano bridge strings out its chainlink
of stars/ glittering notions
blurs of flashing carlights
rippling motions

& from here across the sound's
waters the shore of brooklyn comes alive with yellow
lights that glow
like eyes of panthers

headlights shutter/ blink
down freeways carved from blood & stolen gold
while the american flag shivers/ whips back
hung up there atop staten island's
city hall tower
alone in the face of ice
cold winds
black hands on the white face
of the luminous tower clock
move methodically

while under the bridge
the strung-out motion red
lights pulsate like heartbeats
of a rebreathing bag/ dreams
rise & fall against the darkness
blood colors
bloodshot eyes in flight
feverish eyes of countless rodents
impressionistic images swirling
penetrate the dark rhythms

while down at the ferry landing
cars move like monstrous bugs
down long curving rampways
headlight tongues for eyes probe/ open up
the darkness with their bone bright keys of light
crawl up the snaking asphalt pavement
while people move in slow
fast shuffling motion as in old homemade
silent movies in black & white dragging
their day behind them
anchored to tired drooping shoulders

now across the sound
in the other direction towards manhattan
the eye locates the oxidized green french
woman carved from stone lighting her torch
in the harbor
while manhattan looms up behind her
a gigantic electric circus
of sizzling lights

now night closes in finally
its walls of mystery like dracula
enfolding himself up in his black sweeping cape
while all around staten island supper smells
tantalize the nostrils

now as eye am leaving
the wind dies
down up on the flagpole the flag hangs limply
while black hands on the white face of the clock
turn around the hours fast as jessie owens
winning the olympic dashes
in hitler's germany in 1936

now panther against the dark
eye enter the ferry
slip down through the womb of its doors
like a letter being slid into
an envelope

slides back into the night
postmarked; manhattan

WINTER NIGHT LYRIC

night breathing in winter
chewing at the window
razor-bladed winds
whip soft falling snow
rip heads from shivering shoulders
cause them to sink
into walking overcoats

snow crunch of tire wheels
scream of slipping feet drifting
here & there strangers
leaning against their loneliness
like palm trees bowing
in the hurricane surge

comic images whirl
across television screens locked
behind polished glass squared
in concrete phallic peaks of the decaying
apple flashes its neon brightness
as snow tires chained
dig in   scrape
the whistling frozen night

& we come to the freeze
of sudden winter language
silent the asphalt tomb now
of human speech disintegrating
like flesh in the molding casket
in the hardening ground
the spirit of creation
the constant cyclic process
where change is always constant

& we hear the machete wind
howling like a baying timber wolf
beneath the cold moon laughter
branches like skeletal fingers
of the frozen north land
where we peep the ice cold stars
isolated   like our speech
in the dark whistling vault

& above new york city
the terrifying piercing scream
of police sirens
the lonely wail of an ambulance
the death bark
of gunshots cracking the dark

so as the night is always
here changing   moving   blending
rhythms within the process
of bewildering things

so the teeth of winter
freezes our bewilderment fascinating
chewing outside our windows

speaking a bewitching hymn

THE OLD PEOPLE SPEAK OF DEATH
For Leona Smith, my grandmother

the old people speak of death
frequently now
my grandmother speaks of those now
gone to spirit
now less than bone

they speak of shadows
that graced their days made lovelier
by their wings of light speak of years
& corpses of years of darkness
& of relationships buried
deeper even than residue of bone
gone now beyond hardness
gone now beyond form

they smile now from ingrown roots
of beginnings of those who have left us
& climbed back through the holes the old folks
left in their eyes
for them to enter through

eye walk back now with this poem
through the holes the old folks left in their eyes
for me to enter through walk back to where
eye see them there
the ones that have gone beyond hardness
the ones that have gone beyond form
see them there
darker than where roots began
& lighter than where they go
with their spirits
heavier than stone their memories
sometimes brighter than the flash
of sudden lightning

but green branches will grow
from these roots darker than time
& blacker than even the ashes of nations
sweet flowers will sprout
& wave their love-stroked language
in sun-tongued morning's shadow
the spirit in all our eyes

they have gone now back
to shadow as eye climb back out
from the holes of these old folks eyes
those spirits who sing through this poem
gone now back with their spirits
to fuse with greenness
enter stones & glue their invisible
faces upon the transmigration of earth
nailing winds singing guitar blues
voices through the ribcages
of these days
gone now to where the years run
darker than where roots begin
greener than what they bring

the old people speak of death
frequently now
my grandmother speaks of those now
gone to spirit
now less than bone

LEAVING LOS ANGELES

leaving on the freeway eye thought
of complexity forming los angeles
molding sun shaping rhythms of movements
in streets   sounds
sun on the people
dazzling beauty of women driving music through
new blues dues smog burning the sun hours leaning
dark against mountains in the distance
eternally powerful embracing
the valley carved from stone & stretched out
over colors images freaks unknown & spaced out
hollywood tinsel town wilshire
the beverly hill-billies of feeling
east of fifth street
death hopes
of hobos dripping from wine-slashed faces
freeways wrecked with cars holding the foundation
of rhythm driven by salt of the ocean
forming the scope of the possible
that can be beautiful
as the bird
calling dolphy wondrous flute
song shining amongst the lyrical
sea fingers
spraying water sounds airy
dancing rhythms painting trances
blending sweet new juba spells leap
into weaving sounds of hoodoo mystery
drummed into skies of distance
of vibrations spinning
& gliding

& Wes played the saddest beauty
over heart-bled guitar strings thumbed
as Trane's black face is sun juju shining in eclipse
on the other side of time's rainbow where music
like torrential tears ride grim years
over fears hiccupping
blood/ drops
from black mama's swollen eyes
that run like slaughtered ducks through opium dreams
& wolves slobbering rabid in pentagon dens guard
the drained vision of an empty skullbone
pitted staring holy eyes empty
as america's tired promise of freedom-jive

but out in the streets   sounds
sun toning the flesh-kissed curves
of sugar brown love women
so dazzlingly sweet the beauty
of these women driving new music
through these dues

LEGON, GHANA, AFTER DARK

soft voices invisible serenade
from roadways, courtyards,
laughing trees & serene ponds palming
flat wide green leaves
holding incredibly loud bullfrogs
croaking over motion
of silent goldfish

Ga language sings over
darkening shadows mixing Akan where
English is pushed back into corners
of the language gumbo style

crickets orchestrate
their deafening oracular melodies,
blend high-life rhythms & C. K. Mann
with afro-sound of Fela Ransome Kuti
rumbling ground & a lonely
car horn

music, life's music,
punctuates the sweetness
of this beautiful modal cadence,
lifts the spirit into rare ecstasy

now listening to sculptors
of ancestral root music arranging
& rearranging their perfect chords
& octaves of discord & accord, dissonant
counterpoint eye begin to fall into the black
inkwell that leads to the egg-yoke
on the blue plate of God's table

fall into deep & untroubled sleep
at Akuafo Hall, at the University of Ghana
under rare dark incense showers under
rare dark incense showers

GHANAIAN SONG — IMAGE

after rain
dark trees &
ghost shadows
sit upon
shoulders of
cotton mist

IGBOBI NIGHT;
for Ron & Ellen Pulleyblank & Seyi Bajilayia

dark fall
african masks
martell bottle
shadows
the wall   spider
in the corner
of the cognac
bottle a lone candle
burns on the table
invisible sounds
hum from imagbon
street climbs through
the open window
& love in
the heart will last
beyond distance
& time beyond
separation
of the grave

MEMORY

a lone candle
burning penetrating
the dark deepening
memory — pain
only a finger-
thought away

OUT HERE WHERE

out here where
the sky grows wings
the land is broad
& everywhere eye go
space holds me
within

IT IS NOT

it is not who or what
you see
but how you see
it. the night.

the woman. the rhythm
of night lights going on.
off. in her face.
the smile of neon.
jewels on fingers.

the sound of ash
colliding with cotton.
the sound tears make falling
through blues. the voices.
guitar strings strummed
by silence. echoes.

echoes. gold-capped
dues of a mississippi black
man's grin. is. not who or what.
you see. but how.
you see it. thin.
or otherwise. deep.

this life is.
what you make it. not
what you hope it to be. but
what it is. right or wrong.
what it is what you make it
to be it is right
or wrong. thin.
or otherwise. deep.
a blues. or its absence.
it is. a lyrical

rhythm. dissonant.
painting the night. the sound
of ashes. colliding with cotton.
is. how you hear it. feel it.
is. not what or who.
you either hear. or. you do
not hear. but how you hear
is the question here.

this poem. that gold-
capped blues. of that. black
man's grin. mississippi. is.
the sound tears make falling
through guitar strings.
colliding with cotton.

echoing bones
that lay screaming under-
water. under earth. is
the feeling you hear. chains.
is not what you see
but how you see it. death.
this life. is how you
make it. see it.

feeling. see it. hear
this life wedded to death.
see it. feeling. see it.

feeling. see it.
see. it.
hear. it.

IN A SILENCE OF BELLS

in a silence of bells
& cardboard mackmen
round midnight
a screaming riot of trumpets
fork the suffocating hour

bones stretch
& are hands of time-clocks
beating hearts with no bodies
surrounding them stall in
an absence of rhythms

but eye come in on time
with no help from metronomes
picking bass strings of the night
but have forgotten
my subway token

so have to walk
the music all
the way home

ON A NEW YORK STREET CORNER

sounds of four-four time
being played by a blind black
man jingling coins ringing
silver blood coins
in a battered tin cup on a street
corner in mid-town manhattan a blood
black blue black blind man nailed
to a wooden white cane noddin
off behind dark shades
a black kansas city-styled man
a new york city street blind man
holdin a battered tin cup
playin four-four time
playin kansas city bird prez
count four-four time head noddin
diggin the music of nineteen hundred
& ice cold thirty-four
a blood black man
a blue black blind black
man on a new york street corner
beboppin in time beboppin on down
grinnin a gold tooth crown
& a small head noddin
crowd gathered diggin
on his music

IN MEMORY OF BUNCHY CARTER

in this quick breath
of water spray airy
eye see your face
of light so darkly lit
through knifing
rain long gone friend
shadow of your tracking
tongue still moving
this pain of lost friend-
ship to call out your name
so distant now
so night grown green
under avalanches
of sunlight
& flowers

MAGICAL ENCOUNTER

in central park you move
towards me the summer day
(w)rapping breeze softly

your gingham dress streaked
with taffeta around your lyrical
lithe body
                & you are lathering my body
down with your glowing magical eyes
you move through & into
the light of my dumb-
struck perception
falling through the trees

& then you are gone
like a sunset gone
into the sea

but eye am struck alive
by the whispering cooing sweetness
of your now invisible presence
am struck dumb
by your sundown flesh gone
where choirs of the park whisper
& linger
your perfumed breath
kisses my eyes sad
at your leaving

YOUR PRESENCE

your presence shivers there

where light trails off at the edge
of shadows

& in a miracle
of rainbows & dazzling feathers suddenly
daybreak rings in its bell-tones

a pandemonium of ruptures

flowers all over the sky

THE OTHER NIGHT

the other brandy
sweetened night we was
kissin so hard & good
you sucked my tongue
right on out
my tremblin mouth
& eye had to
sew it back in
in order to tell
you about it

FOURTEEN LINES FOR "WARM"

eye am combing through my memories
with a fine tooth-comb of recall, as if
they were so many strands of hair, like pages

of years flicking swiftly as film

& now eye see you & am next to you there
little girl blue where the blood is screaming
scary beneath my window

in the street there in the bed now
where your face is all wrapped tight in pain

shadows growing wings in your eyes
while eye am coming someone else is leaving
as the doors of your eyes slam shut

this day's flames drop dead as sunsets
deep illumination screws stars into the night

FLYING KITES
(For Nathan Dixon, Friend & Poet)

1.

we used to fly kites
across skull-caps of hours
holes on blue wings
canvas of sinking suns eclipsed
winged eyes locked to wind
we'd cut the kite string away
then run them down blue tapestry
up the sky down again the sin-
king sun over
again the sinking sun

2.

now we fly words as kites
on winds through skies
as poems;
holy bloody sounds
ringing like eclipse
the sun's tongues

TRANSFORMATION

catch the blues song
of wind in your bleeding
black hand, (w)rap it around
your strong bony fingers
then turn it into a soft-nosed pen
& sit down & write the love
poem of your life

FIREFLIES

fireflies on night canvas
cat eyes glowing like moonbeams
climbing now towards hidden places
they speak to the language
of darkness & of their lives torn
from roots in flux & of their sub-
stance forming the core
substantially transparent they
swim through ethereal darkness
where silence can be wisdom
searching for open doors

THE DAY DUKE RAISED; may 24th, 1974
For Duke Ellington

1.

that day began with a shower
of darkness calling lightning rains
home to stone language
of thunderclaps shattering the high
blue elegance of space & time
a broken-down riderless horse
with frayed wings
rode a sheer bone sunbeam
road down into the clouds

2.

spoke wheels of lightning
spun around the hours high up
above those clouds duke wheeled
his chariot of piano keys
his spirit now levitated from flesh
& hovering over the music of most high
spoke to the silence
of a griot shaman/ man
who knew the wisdom of God

3.

at high noon the sun cracked
through the darkness like a rifle shot
grew a beard of clouds on its livid bald
face hung down noon sky high
pivotal time of the flood-deep hours as duke
was pivotal being a five in the nine
numbers of numerology
as his music was the crossroads
the cosmic mirror of rhythmic gri-gri

4.

so get on up & fly away duke bebop
slant & fade on in strut dance swing riff
float & stroke those tickling gri-gri keys
those satin ladies taking the A train up
to harlem those gri-gri keys of birmingham
breakdown sophisticated
ladies mood indigo
so get on up & strut across gri-gri
raise on up your band's waiting

5.

thunderclapping music somersaulting
clouds racing across the blue deep wisdom
of God listen it is time for your intro
duke into that other place where the all-time
great band is waiting for your intro duke
it is time for the Sacred Concert duke
it is time to make the music of God
duke we are listening for your intro
duke let the sacred music begin

FOUR, AND MORE; for Miles Davis

1.

a carrier of incandescent dreams this
blade-thin shadowman stabbed by lightning
crystal silhouette
crawling over blues-stained pavements his life
lean he drapes himself his music across edges
his blood held tight within
staccato flights

clean as darkness & bright as lightning
reversed moments where the sound is two cat eyes
penetrating the midnight hours of moon pearls lacing
the broken mirrored waters
mississippi mean as a sun-drenched trumpet/ man
holding dreams held high on any wind/ light

voice walking on eggshells

2.

& time comes as the wrinkles
of your mother's skin shrinking inward
fly towards that compelling voice
light calling since time began
on the flip-side of spirit
you shed placentas at each stage of your music
then go down river exploring new blues

the drum skin of young years wearing down

the enigmatic search of your music
now your autumn years of shadows creeping twilight
dancers wrapped tight in cobwebs hold on
to one another
beneath fractured lights cracking the floor
their lives now prismatic poems at the point where the sun
disappears with every turning of the clock hands
spinning towards the death of light
there in the diamond point
of the river beyond the edges

the light glows smaller
grows inward becomes a seed to grow
another light illuminating the shadows
crystalline as this trumpetman

voice walking on eggshells

phosphorous as truth or blue
as luminescent water beneath the sun's eye

3.

O Silent Keeper of Shadows
of these gutted roads filled with gloomy ticking
of time-clocks/ razor-bladed turnings of hairpin corners
of these irreducible moments of love found
when love was sought
irridescent keeper of rainbow laughter
arching out of broken-off gold-capped teeth

blues man holding the sun between his teeth

soothsayer of chewed-up moments
shekereman at the crossroads of cardinal points
talisman hanging from dewdrops singing deep
sea diver of transparent rhythmic poems

trumpet voice walking on eggshells

your shadow is as the river snake-thin
man at flood time blood lengthening in the veins
coursing through the earth's flesh

shaman man gone beyond the skies limit

music sleeps there in the riverbed
mississippi where those calcified shining bones sleep
deep reminding us of the journey from then to now
& from now to wherever it is we have to go

so pack your bags boy
the future is right around the corner
only a stone's throw from yesterday's/ light

as is this carrier of afternoon dream music
trumpet voice walking on eggshells

this eggshell-walking trumpetman
voice hauntingly beautiful lyrical music man
gold as two cat eyes penetrating the midnight hours
as blood blackening the pavement mean music man
shadowman holding the night in the bell
of his trumpet singing

mississippi river pouring from roots of his eyes

4.

shadowman holding the night in his music
shekereman at the crossroads of cardinal points
elliptical talisman hanging from dewdrops singing
deep sea diver of haunting magical tones

trumpetman walking on eggshells

your shadow as the river at flood-time
snake-thin shaman man blade-sharp gone beyond
the skies limit music sleeps there in your coursing
river veins curl around the bones
clear as diamond points on waters of sunsets

there where light grows inward
your genius moving out from that source
trumpetman walking on eggshells

afternoon dreamcarrier of blues in flight
steep night climber of haunting magical poems

juju hoodooman conjuring illuminating darkness

SNAKE-BACK SOLO
(For Louis Armstrong, Steve Cannon, Miles Davis & Eugene Redmond)

with the music up high
boogalooin bass down way way low
up & under eye come slidin on in mojoin
on in spacin on in on a riff
full of rain
riffin on in full of rain & pain
spacin on in on a sound like coltrane

my metaphor is a blues
hot pain dealin blues is a blues axin
guitar voices whiskey broken niggah deep
in the heart is a blues in a glass filled with rain
is a blues in the dark
slurred voices of straight bourbon
is a blues dagger stuck off in the heart
of night moanin like bessie smith
is a blues filling up the wings
of darkness is a blues

& looking through the heart
a dream can become a raindrop window to see through
can become a window to see through this moment
to see yourself hanging around the dark
to see through
can become a river catching rain
feeding time can become a window
to see through

while outside windows flames trigger
the deep explosion
time steals rivers that go on & stay where they are
inside yourself moving soon there will be daylight
breaking the darkness
to show the way soon there will be voices breaking music
to come on home by down & up river breaking darkness
swimming up river the sound of louie armstrong
carrying riverboats upstream on vibratos
climbing the rain filling the rain
swimming up river
up the river of rain satchmo breaking the darkness
his trumpet & grin polished overpain speaking
to the light flaming off the river's back
at sunset snake river's back
river mississippi big muddy up from new
orleans to alton & east st. louis illinois
cross the river from st. louis to come on home by
up river the music swims breaking silence of miles
flesh leaping off itself into space
creating music creating poems

now inside myself eye solo of rivers
catching rains & dreams & sunsets solo
of trane tracks screaming through night stark
a dagger in the heart solo
of the bird spreading wings for the wind
solo of miles pied piper prince of darkness
river rain voice now eye solo
at the root of the flower solo leaning voices
against promises of shadows soloing of bones
beneath the river's snake-back solo
of trees cut down by double-bladed axes
river rain voice now eye solo of the human condition
as blues solo of the matrix mojoin new blues solo
river rain voice now eye solo   solo

& looking through the heart a dream
can become a raindrop window to see through
can become this moment this frame to see through
to see yourself hanging
around the dark to see through this pain
can become even more painful as the meaning of bones
crawling mississippi river bottoms snakepits beneath
the snake-back solo catching rain catching time
& dreams washed clean by ajax

but looking through the dream can be
like looking through a clean window crystal
prism the night where eye solo now too be-
come the wings of night
to see through this darkness
eye solo now to become wings & colors
to become a simple skybreak shattering darkness
to become lightning's jagged sword-like thunder
eye solo to become to become
eye solo now to become to become

with the music up high
up way way high boogalooin bass down
way way low
up & under eye come slidin on in mojoin on in
spacin on in on a riff full of rain
river riff full of rain & trains & dreams
come slidin on in another riff
full of flames
leanin & glidin eye solo solo
loopin & slidin eye solo now solo

POEM FOR SKUNDER BOGHASSIAN, PAINTER

music drumming skies
of your paintings of poetry
miles cookin there
with long gone trane leapin
canopies of distance

& space can be canvas
or bark negotiated by brushstrokes of silence

ghost evoking illusions of myth
wind-voice gongs
shaping shadows from mist

signatures that echo

COLLAGE

wings of snow sweep
disintegrate
slow fall chimney ashes
belch through gray night
silently screaming

voices thick as molasses

blanket fluttering pavements
slide into one another
below moments
faces

ringing like bells

DUSK SONG: PHOTOGRAPH
(For Chester Higgins, Photographer)

here american indigo wings
pulsating electric sable descending
the sun
in talons of screaming hawks here
we await the comet kahoutek's passing
close to a frozen sun

evening dusk songs
descending gongs in africa baobab tree black
sculpture of beauty inked snapped
lithograph
of fire wagon red set
against screaming illuminosity
of jaundiced sun stark
hanging up there
a lyrical silence
a throbbing syllable

poetic pulsating space disc
luminous dusk song gong
golden coin flashed on fire wagon red sky
photographed eye precise
by chester higgins

hung up there in space
beyond place
& time this beautiful echo
frozen xanthous in pulsating red space
beyond trace
this golden echo
frozen above baobab tree black

MY POEMS HAVE HOLES SEWN INTO THEM

my poems have holes sewn into them
& they run searching for light
at the end of tunnels they become trains
or at the bottom of pits they become blackness
or in the broad winging daylight
they are the words that fly

& the holes are these words
letters or syllables with feathered wings
that leave their marks on white pages
then fly off like footprints tracked in snow
& only God knows where they go

this poem has holes stitched into it
as our speech which created poetry in the first place
lacerated wounded words that strike out original
meaning bleeding into language
hemorrhaging out of thick or thin mouths
has empty spaces & silences sewn into it

so my poems have holes sewn into them
& their voices are like different keyholes
through which dumb men search for speech blind
men search for sight
words like drills penetrating sleep
keys turning in the keyholes of language
like knives of sunrays stabbing blind eyes

my poems have holes sewn into them
& they are the spaces between words
are the words themselves
falling off into one another/ colliding
like people gone mad they space out
fall into bottomless pits
which are the words

like silent space between chords of a piano
or black eyes of a figure in any painting
they fall back into themselves
into time/ sleep
bottom out on the far side of consciousness
where words of all the worlds poets go
& whisper in absolute silence

this poem has deep holes stitched into it
& their meanings have the deadly suck of quicksand
the irreversible pull of earth to any skydiver
the tortured pus-holes in arms of junkies

my poems have holes sewn into them
& they run searching for light at the end
of tunnels or at the bottom of yawning pits
or in the broad daylight where
the words flapping like wings of birds
fly whispering in absolute silence